Animal Worlds

Animals in the Wild

Sue Barraclough

Raintree

Chicago, Illinois

Customer Service   888–454–2279

Visit our website at www.heinemannlibrary.com

Photo research by Ruth Blair and Kay Altwegg
Designed by Jo Hinton-Malivoire and bigtop design ltd
Printed and bound in China by South China Printing Company

10 09 08 07 06
10 9 8 7 6 5 4 3 2 1

Library of Congress Cataloging-in-Publication Data
Barraclough, Sue.
  Animals in the wild / Sue Barraclough.
    p. cm. -- (Animal worlds)
  ISBN 1-4109-1896-3 (library binding - hardcover) -- ISBN 1-4109-1901-3 (pbk.)
  1. Animals--Juvenile literature. I. Title. II. Series: Barraclough, Sue. Animal worlds.
  QL49.B258 2005
  590--dc22
                              2005006757
Acknowledgments
The author and publisher are grateful to the following for permission to reproduce copyright
material: Corbis pp. 9, 18, 19; FLPA p. 17; FLPA/David Hosking p. 13; FLPA/Frans
Lanting/Minden Pictures pp. 10, 16; FLPA/Frits Van Daalen/Foto Natura p. 6; FLPA/Gerard
Lacz p. 17, 19; FLPA/Hannu Hautala p. 11; FLPA/Michio Hoshino/Minden Pictures p. 20;
FLPA/Panda Photo p. 7; FLPA/Terry Whittaker p. 23; FLPA/Yva Momatiuk & John
Eastcott/Minden Pictures p. 12; Getty Images/Digital Vision p. 14; NHPA/Jonathan & Angela
Scott p. 22; NHPA/Melvin Grey p. 21; NHPA/Michael Leach p. 8; OSF pp. 4, 5.

Cover photograph reproduced with permission of photolibrary.com/osf.

Some words are shown in bold, **like this**. You can find out
what they mean by looking in the glossary.

Contents

Animals in the Wild

There are lots of different wild animals.

Wild animals have to find food and water. These animals have come for a drink.

This elephant drinks water through its **trunk**.

Different Wild Animals

Wild animals come in all shapes and sizes.

This big bear lives in the mountains.

Squirrels live in many different places.

Do you know what squirrels like to eat?

Nests and Burrows

Some wild animals make their homes underground.

Rabbits live in homes called **burrows**.

This animal is called
a raccoon. It makes its
nest high up in a tree.

Food and Water

MUNCH
MUNCH

Wild animals need food to stay healthy.

Giraffes have long necks to reach leaves high in the trees.

All animals need water to drink. This bird drinks from a pool.

Animals in the Air

Some animals have wings and can fly.

Bats fly around at night.

Many birds fly in big groups called **flocks**.

What do you think these gulls are looking for?

Animals in the Water

Some wild animals live underwater.

14

These fish live in the ocean. They swim around the **coral** to look for food.

Moving Around

Kangaroos have strong back legs for hopping along.

boING!

Orangutans have long arms for swinging through trees.

Dolphins use their tails to push them through the water.

17

Making Noises

Wild animals make all kinds of noises.

Wolves howl.

ow-ow-OWWW!

Tigers growl.

GRRRRR!

Can you squawk like a parrot?

SQUAWK!

19

Baby Wild Animals

Animals take care of their babies.

These polar bear cubs stay close to their mother.

Birds find food for their young.

This bird caught a caterpillar
for her babies to eat.

Caring and Cleaning

Wild animals take good care of each other.

Lions use their tongues to lick their fur clean.

Baboons use their fingers to clean each other.

Glossary

burrow home underground where an animal lives

coral tiny ocean animal that lives in groups.

flock group of birds

trunk part of an elephant's body that is used to pick things up

Index

Notes for adults

Animal Worlds investigates a variety of animals by looking at their distinguishing features and characteristics and by exploring their different environments.

This series supports a young child's knowledge and understanding of their world. The books are designed to help children extend their vocabulary as they are introduced to new words. Words are used in context in each book to enable young children to gradually incorporate them into their own vocabulary.

Follow-up activities:

Encourage children to think about any wild animals they have seen in parks and gardens, and to draw a picture of their favorite animal and where it lives.